Published by Creative Education
and Creative Paperbacks
P.O. Box 227, Mankato, Minnesota 56002
Creative Education and Creative Paperbacks
are imprints of The Creative Company
www.thecreativecompany.us

Design by The Design Lab
Production by Travis Green
Art direction by Rita Marshall
Printed in the United States of America

Photographs by Corbis (Theo Allofs, Nigel Pavitt/JAI,
Anup Shah, Winfried Wisniewski/Minden Pictures),
Dreamstime (Michele Alfieri, Andreanita, Janina Kubik,
Duncan Noakes, Boaz Yunior Wibowo), iStockphoto
(KurtJayBertels), Shutterstock (Stanislav Popov, Villiers
Steyn, Johan Swanepoel)

Library of Congress Cataloging-in-Publication Data
Riggs, Kate.
Antelopes / Kate Riggs.
p. cm. — (Amazing animals)
Summary: A basic exploration of the appearance,
behavior, and habitat of antelopes, the bovids of
Africa and Asia. Also included is a story from folklore
explaining how tsessebes got their horns.
Includes bibliographical references and index.
ISBN 978-1-60818-608-2 (hardcover)
ISBN 978-1-62832-214-9 (pbk)
ISBN 978-1-56660-655-4 (eBook)
1. Antelopes—Juvenile literature. I. Title. II. Series:
Amazing animals.
QL737.U53R544 2016
599.64—dc23   2014048699

CCSS: RI.1.1, 2, 4, 5, 6, 7; RI.2.2, 5, 6, 7, 10;
RI.3.1, 5, 7, 8; RF.1.1, 3, 4; RF.2.3, 4

First Edition HC 9 8 7 6 5 4 3 2 1
First Edition PBK 9 8 7 6 5 4 3 2 1

AMAZING ANIMALS
ANTELOPES

BY KATE RIGGS

Peachtree

CREATIVE EDUCATION • CREATIVE PAPERBACKS

Impalas are antelopes that live on the African savannas

Antelopes are African and Asian animals. There are almost 100 kinds of antelopes! Some live in grasslands called savannas. Some live in woods and forests. And some live in deserts like the Sahara.

savannas flat, hot lands covered with grass and a few trees

Antelopes are animals known as bovids. Cows, sheep, and bison are bovids, too. Bovids have hooves and horns. An antelope's fur is short and stiff like a brush.

Elands have a strip of longer, darker hair called a mane on their backs

The giant eland is the largest antelope. Male elands can weigh 2,000 pounds (907 kg). Royal antelopes weigh seven pounds (3.2 kg). They are only as tall as a piece of paper! They can hide in the bushes.

A blue duiker may be no bigger than a house cat

The color of their fur helps other antelopes hide. Some antelopes have white stripes or markings on their fur. Kudus have white stripes that wrap around their bodies.

Light, striped fur helps kudus blend in with grasses and brush

Antelopes eat plants like acacia and bamboo. Gerenuks stand on their back legs to reach tall bushes. Other antelopes eat grasses and short plants.

Gerenuks stretch their necks and pull down high branches

Young wildebeest run up to 40 miles (64.4 km) per hour

A doe has one or two **calves** at a time. The calves drink milk from their mother. Wildebeest can run on the savanna 15 minutes after birth. Antelope calves in the woods stay in one spot for a long time. They hide from **predators**.

calves baby antelopes

doe a female antelope

predators animals that kill and eat other animals

Antelopes can live for 15 to 25 years. Most live together in groups. Small groups are called bands. A herd is made up of many bands. Hundreds or thousands of antelopes live in a herd. The herd travels to find food.

Herds of wildebeest try to stay away from predators

Antelopes spend a lot of time eating or looking for food. Gazelles and wildebeest walk a long way to find food. Some antelopes get the water they need from plants. Others need to drink more water.

Some antelopes gather at desert watering holes to drink

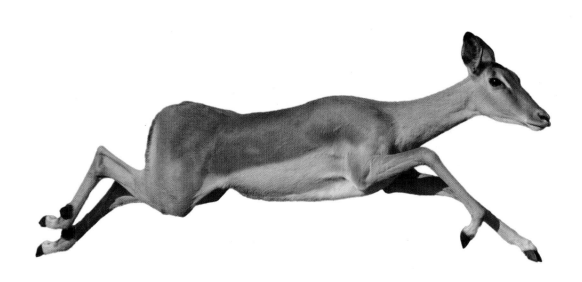

People in Africa make masks that look like antelopes. They wear the masks as they dance. Outside Africa, many antelopes live in zoos. People love watching these graceful animals run!

In Mali, the Dogon people wear antelope masks called walu

An Antelope Story

Do all antelopes have horns? People in Africa told a story about the tsessebe (*TAY-seh-bee*) antelope. Tsessebe was once the only antelope without horns. He was very sad. The only horns left were ugly bones, but Tsessebe did not care. He put them on anyway. Now he was the fastest antelope, and he had his own horns!

Read More

Gates, Margo. *Antelopes*. Minneapolis: Bellwether Media, 2014.

Stewart, Melissa. *Antelope*. Danbury, Conn.: Children's Press, 2002.

Websites

Enchanted Learning: Antelopes
http://www.enchantedlearning.com/subjects/mammals/antelope/Antelopecoloring.shtml
This site has facts about the antelope and a picture to color.

Make Your Own Antelope Horns
http://www.calacademy.org/teachers/resources/lessons/make-your-own-antelope-horns/
Have an adult help you follow the steps to make horns that look like an antelope's!

Note: Every effort has been made to ensure that the websites listed above are suitable for children, that they have educational value, and that they contain no inappropriate material. However, because of the nature of the Internet, it is impossible to guarantee that these sites will remain active indefinitely or that their contents will not be altered.